RUBY McMIKE

KINDLE INCOME

The Ultimate Guide On How to Make Money from
Kindle, Discover Everything You Need to Know About
Kindle Publishing and How to Profit From It

Descrierea CIP a Bibliotecii Naționale a României
RUBY McMIKE
    KINDLE INCOME. The Ultimate Guide On How to Make Money from Kindle, Discover Everything You Need to Know About Kindle Publishing and How to Profit From It / Ruby McMike – Bucharest: Editura My Ebook, 2020
    ISBN

RUBY McMIKE

KINDLE INCOME

The Ultimate Guide On How to Make Money from
Kindle, Discover Everything You Need to Know About
Kindle Publishing and How to Profit From It

My Ebook Publishing House
Bucharest, 2020

TABLE OF CONTENTS

INTRODUCTION...

Kindle has become huge over the last few years. Everywhere you go you see people holding their Kindle's and being engrossed in their reading... and it has become equally as popular as an online business model. People from all around the world have written ebooks and turned themselves into published authors - and in this report we're going to discuss why it's become so popular and how you can join them too.

You might not see yourself as an author - but as we're going to discuss writing a book doesn't have to be as difficult as you might imagine. The truth is that Kindle can be a great business to get into for many people - and as well as having the fun of seeing your book on the virtual shelves it can also be extremely lucrative too.

Without further ado let's get into it...

WHY HAS KINDLE BECOME SO POPULAR WITH USERS?

Whether you're on a train, bus or sitting in the park you're always seeing people reading their Kindle. Quite honestly it is MASSIVE - and it's probably only going to get even more so over the next few years.

But why has it become so popular?

When the idea of e-readers first came about many people scoffed at the concept and said that they wouldn't take off because people would always prefer reading from a traditional book. They argued that part of the reading experience is turning the pages and seeing lots of books on your shelves at home.

Perhaps a key reason for Kindle's popularity is that you can store an entire library of books on one small, portable device. It doesn't matter whether you've got 2 books or 100 books stored on your Kindle - it'll still take up exactly the same amount of space in your bag, meaning that you can take your entire book collection with you wherever you go.

Along a similar line is that with a Kindle you can purchase a book at the touch of a button. Let's say you are browsing the internet one day and come across a new book that you really want to read. Before the days of Kindle you would have to order it and wait for it to be delivered - or you would need to pop to the shops and pick up yourself a copy. With a Kindle you can purchase the book at a touch of a button and have it sitting on your device just a minute later.

Of course there ARE some disadvantages to Kindle...

Books with lots of images, for example, can be better when you've got a hard copy, however in recent years Kindle has come up with their Fire devices to combat this somewhat. These Kindle's are now fully functioning tablet computers that compete with devices such as Apple's iPad, thus introducing Kindle to a whole new audience and expanding the possibilities considerably.

FOUR REASONS WHY YOU SHOULD GET INTO KINDLE

As we have mentioned, publishing on Kindle is a very popular phenomenon nowadays. Multiple writers are opting to get into Kindle to publish their books. But why should YOU get into Kindle?

Well, here are four good reasons...

You are in control of your publishing fate

Publishing on Kindle is the best mode of self publishing you can have. If you try to publish in the traditional way, then you might have to wait for months and years to get your manuscript approved and to get a good deal in publishing the book. In the world of publishing, the more you wait, the more money you lose. This issue is taken care of if you opt for Kindle publishing. Here, since you are self publishing the book, you do not have to waste too much time over running from one publishing house to another. You also have the control over making changes to the book whenever you need to.

Kindle publishing is easy

Publishing on Kindle is as easy as it gets. You can get started whenever you wish to and publish your book on Kindle. The tools provided are simple to understand. All you have to do is write out your book on MS Word and then follow some simple steps to publish it. You can publish your book, along with necessary formatting and editing, in just half and hour. It cannot get easier than this!

You get decent royalty

Hundreds of people are opting for Kindle not just for its convenience of publishing or worldwide reach. Kindle also gives you the opportunity to earn very good royalty on your published ebooks. So, if you thought that publishing on Kindle would be a monetary loss, then you are mistaken.

You can reach a wide audience

People spend more time online than they do anywhere else. We are digitally connected all the time - so, it makes sense to publish your book on a digital platform where thousands of people log in everyday to check what's new. You can instantly market your book worldwide. Hence, if you get into Kindle and publish your book, then you will get instant access to the huge digital crowd and thereby reap the benefits.

THE KINDLE ADVANTAGE

Reading will never be out of fashion. Hence, writers will always find their place on the reader's shelves, if only they can reach them.

Years ago becoming a published writer meant going in circles from one publishing house to another and depositing copies of your manuscript for them to read. It would take months and often years to get the manuscript approved, edited and published into books.

The same process still exists of course - but with Kindle it can be much easier...

Kindle books take less time to publish

Think about the months that you might have to spend trying to convince a publishing house to publish your book.

Now think about publishing that book of yours in ebook form in under an hour...

Which seems to be a better option?

One of the biggest advantages of Kindle publishing lies in the fact that you will not have to be at the mercy of publishing houses to get your book published. This is a huge benefit as losing time is equal to losing money in the publishing world. You do not even have to be a tech expert to publish your book in Kindle. You can just write out your book in MS Word. Once on Kindle you can simply follow the instructions given there to edit and format your file. Thereafter, you can publish your ebook. And all this is a super fast process. So, your book is out there in the market sooner and within the reach of all your potential readers.

Kindle books are easier to market than hard copy book

When you publish a hard copy book with a publishing house, the house takes the responsibility of marketing the book through various book launches and interviews and book parties. But, if you are on your own and are thinking about self publishing your book, then marketing might be the biggest hurdle you will encounter.

However, if you decide to publish a Kindle ebook, then your marketing troubles will be simplified by a large extent...

On the digital platform, it is easier to spread the word. The moment you publish a book on Kindle, it becomes accessible to thousands and thousands of readers. Hence, your book can have worldwide reach within hours of publishing on Kindle – something that hard copy books cannot claim to attain so easily. Book publishing has never been this easy or profitable!

HOW TO COME UP WITH IDEAS
FOR KINDLE BOOKS

Ok - so I've convinced you that Kindle is a good way forward. Now it's time to get going and start publishing some books...

But hang on just a minute!

"What can I write? I haven't got any ideas!"

Coming up with good book ideas is a must

In order to be a success on Kindle, your book ideas need to be the best. Everyday numerous authors are publishing books on Kindle. So - in order to compete, you need to have a book idea which will be different and will interest the readers.

Coming up with viable book ideas may seem like an easy concept – but it is not. It takes quite some hard work.

There are indeed particular ways in which you can come up with decent ideas for Kindle books...

Do your research!

One of the best ways of starting your research is having a dig around in the Kindle store. Here you will find lists of bestsellers that have been tremendously successful. So, there must be something in these book ideas that worked with the readers. Hence, a good way to come up with good ideas for Kindle book is to research more on what has already worked on Kindle...

The best way to do this is by first picking the genre or topic you wish to write on and then going through that particular category or related category of books on Kindle. When you do so, you would find the book descriptions as well as the reader reviews. This will help you research on what kind of books have already been written on the topic and what the readers liked and did not like. This way, you will be able to get good ideas on what exactly your book should be on.

You can also research all over the internet on your chosen genre and any related information. The more you research, the more refined you get in your choice of ideas for your Kindle book.

Keep following trends

Trends come and go - but there are ALWAYS particular topics which are hot at the present time.

So - make it your job to always know what the current trends are.

You will find trends in genres or current topics or even popular incidents. Find out what is popular among readers now, and then modify it according to your style of writing, or the topic of your choice. This way, you can retain your originality while getting new and viable ideas for your Kindle book.

Brainstorm and discuss your ideas

It is easy to feel stressed or overwhelmed when thinking up new ideas for your Kindle book all alone. In times like this, brainstorming can indeed make the task easier for you...

The key to writing a good Kindle book is in finding the perfect niche for yourself. For this, you must soak in as much information as possible from the internet, other books etc. Then discuss it out with your peers, other writers or experts in the fields you wish to write about. The more people you talk to and discuss with, the more ideas you will get.

Think about topics or genres that truly interest you

Although it's important to make sure that your book subject actually has a market (there's obviously no point in writing something nobody is interested in) - it's also worth considering whether you actually have an interest in the topic...

Well written books are the ones which the writer had fun writing. Unless you enjoy the writing process, the book will seem dull or forced - however many writers make the mistake of picking up a genre or topic that they aren't interested in. That's maybe "ok" if you're outsourcing your book writing to a ghostwriter (covered later) - but if you're writing it yourself then it's really no use picking something you actively HATE writing about.

CREATING THE BOOK

By now you've hopefully come up with some ideas for a book and picked a topic.

By the way, don't spend forever and a day making your mind up....

Although it's important to carefully do your research, there has to become a point when you just say "ok, this is what I'm going to write my book about." Many people worry so much about choosing the "right" topic that they never actually make a decision...

Do a reasonable amount of research and then once you're pretty convinced there's some kind of market/interest in the topic then just go with it.

Write it yourself or outsource it?

Ok, so when it comes down to creating your book you can either write it yourself or get someone else to write it for you.

Let's tackle the first one:

Writing it yourself

If you're good at writing then this is the ideal option because it allows you to inject your own personality and experiences into the book.

In addition, wouldn't it be more satisfying to publish a book that you personally wrote?

If you go down this route then you need to make your writing interesting...

Write with personality

Every writer has a certain personality or tone quality, which the reader connects with. The worst thing you can do to your writing is to write in an even, dull tone or try to copy the tone of some other writer. In order to be interesting, your writing must have a voice of its own. Hence, in order to make your

Kindle book more interesting, work on developing a personality for your writing.

Research a lot

If you want to write a well thought out book, you cannot avoid research. Thorough researching is every writer's best friend. As they say in the literary world, God is in the details. You cannot possibly get the details right if you do not research properly. So, make it a point to talk to different people, read a lot and find out more about the topic or genre you wish to write on.

If you're writing a fiction book then develop a good plot with strong characters

The essence of the book is in its plot and characters. Develop an interesting plot that will keep your readers hooked. Create realistic and interesting characters, out of your imagination or interactions with different people. The more you keep your characters relatable, the more interesting your book will be.

Double check spelling and grammar

This is often an underrated point, but the importance of good spelling and grammar is paramount. The moment people discover grammatical or spelling mistakes in your Kindle book, they will write you off as an amateur.

Don't think you're a writer? Here's how to get a Kindle book written without writing it yourself...

Not everyone has the desire or skill to write a book. It certainly takes quite a lot of skill and patience to write an entire book, even if it's relatively short.

The good news however is that you don't have to be a writer in order to take advantage of Kindle. You can earn from publishing books on Kindle, even if you do not write them yourself...

On Kindle, you are, basically, a publisher

In the traditional publishing world, one can easily tell the difference between the writer and the publisher. The writer is the one who puts together a book and submits the manuscript to the publishing house. Here, the publisher is in charge of publishing the book and also making all the marketing and promoting efforts. But, when it comes to Kindle publishing, these lines get blurred. Here, you are self publishing the book. Hence, even if you write the whole thing, you are still responsible for all the marketing or promoting tasks – without which your book will simply not sell. Since, the job mainly needs you to be the publisher, your opportunity to earn without writing is right here.

Get another writer to write your book

Ghostwriting is a very popular service provided by a number of independent writers. In simple terms ghostwriting means that the writer writes the entire book, but does not put his or her name on it. So, you can simply hire a ghostwriter to write a book of whichever topic you wish to. You have to pay the ghostwriter the fee they ask for. Once the final draft is ready, you can publish the book on Kindle.

Make sure the writer you choose does justice to the book. The first few pages of a book is often given as free sample on Kindle, to attract the readers who will read that and want to buy the entire book. In order to sell more books on Kindle, the book itself has to be well written and attractive.

Double your marketing efforts

When you use a ghostwriter you also have better chance of focussing more on the marketing and promotion part. So, focus on giving the book an attractive cover. Have a great title. Discuss about the book on social networking sites, discussion forums and blogs. You can even start a dedicated website for the book. Along with that, decide the price at which you would like to sell the book and the countries where you would want to make it available. This way, you will be able to escalate your sales and earn good money without writing the Kindle book yourself.

Also consider the "half way house..."

What if you want to write the book yourself but you just find the prospect too daunting?

The good news is that there's a third option - and that's to use PLR material as a *starting point.*

PLR is where you purchase the rights to a pre-written ebook or content. These "rights" allow you to change the content, re-write it, add your name as the author and basically sell it as thought it was your own. PLR licenses do vary however, so it's important to check exactly what you are and aren't allowed to do.

IMPORTANT: PLR isn't allowed on Kinde

PLR material actually isn't allowed on Kindle - but that doesn't necessarily mean that you can't use it at all...

You can't use it "as is" - but what about buying a PLR ebook and then completely re-writing it, adding your own experiences, anecdotes etc?

You would need to completely re-write it and make it totally unrecognisable from the original, but that's the best way to use PLR *anyway*. Simply use the PLR material to give you an idea of what to write about!

PUBLISHING YOUR BOOK ON KINDLE

By this stage you've got an ebook that you want to sell on Kindle. Now it's time to publish it...

Formatting and editing your ebook

Before you get into the process of submitting your book on Kindle, you need to get the final draft of the book ready. For this purpose, do a thorough formatting and editing of your book, wherever required. Do the complete grammar and spelling check. Make sure your book format is compatible with Kindle. Kindle accepts MS Word, HTML, MOBI, ePUB, TXT or PDF format. If your book file is in any other format, then change it to one of these formats.

Sign up on the digital text platform

The digital text platform or DTP is what will allow you to publish your book on Amazon Kindle. If you publish your ebook through this platform, it will be available on Kindle for purchase by the readers and you will also be eligible to earn the royalty. Your book will be available on Kindle applications in an array of systems like Android, Windows, Blackberry, Mac etc. So, you need to sign in to the Amazon account. Once you sign in, you will have to provide the complete seller information – since you intend to sell books here. Seller information will include the name of the publusher, your tax information and also the payment information. Once your details are saved, you will be ready for publishing.

Add the book

The next step now is to add the book. Click on the 'add new title' icon and fill out the details of the book. You have to fill out the title of the book, who are the writers and the contributors who helped create the book. Contributors may include illustrators, editors, photographers etc. Thereafter you need to fill in a short description about the book. Lastly, you will need to put in the publishing details of the book – that is, the language in which it is being published, the date on which it is being published, the name of the publisher etc.

Adding the other details

When submitting the Kindle book, there are a lot of other areas that need to be taken care of. You need to upload the cover image. You will need to set the publishing rights for your book. You have to specify whether your book content is of public domain or whether you have necessary copyrights. This will affect the royalty you get from the book. Also, you will have to choose your publishing territories – that is, where in the worldwide network do you want your book to be available. This will affect the sales of your book, as particular countries tend to be a better market for a particular type of book. You also have to set rights of digital management for your book.

Set the pricing

After the above step, next comes pricing. You have to set the price at which you wish to sel the book. You also have to set the royalty.

If your book has public domain publishing right, then it will be eligible for 35% royalty. If it is copyrighted, then it will get 70% royalty. So make your choice accordingly.

Submit the book

Once all the above steps are complete, your book will be ready for submission on Kindle. All you have to do now is click on submit and your book will be submitted. It will go through a review by Amazon first, and if approved, it will be available on Kindle store.

PROMOTING YOUR KINDLE BOOK

Publishing to Kindle is relatively easy, but once it's "out there" you're going to have to market it. Without marketing it's basically like creating a website and expecting visitors to "come to you."

So, in order to be successful, your book also needs to be marketed well. In case of traditional publishing houses, the task of marketing is usually taken up by the house itself. But here, since you are self publishing, the marketing part has to be handled by you.

Given below are five easy ways to promote your Kindle book...

Utilize the social networking sites

There is a reason social network marketing is such a rage today. Almost everyone is active in at least one social networking site today. It is where the buzz about the newest products goes on.

And being talked about on a social networking site is the best thing that can happen to your Kindle book. So, before you even upload the Kindle book, make it a point to set up accounts in these sites and build a good friend list. Sign up in the various forum websites and join in the conversations going on. Make yourself as well acquainted as possible. Once your book is published on Kindle, advertise it on the social networks, include the link in your signature in forums or even emails. Create a Facebook page or tweet about it.

Use your blog

As a publisher, your blog can be one of your biggest weapons to promote your Kindle book.

If you maintain a steady blog, then you would have built up a steady readership too. Advertise your book extensively on your blog. Take good pictures and post them. Make it look like a virtual launch of your Kindle book. You can also promote over video chatting platforms like Skype, or upload a video of it on Youtube and include a link on your blog.

Have a free promotional sale

When you publish your book on Kindle, you often get a limited period promotional free sale. Utilize these days to the fullest. Announce the promotional sale of your Kindle book for free over the social networking sites as well as your own blogging platform. There are also various platforms, which focus only on book and reading like Goodreads. Make sure to promote extensively on these platforms, as you will get much more prospective readers here.

Offer books for review

This is yet another good way of utilizing the digital space for promoting your Kindle book. Books which have reviews are often bought more than the books without any reviews. Reviews mean that the book has been read and recommended by someone. The power of word of mouth plays a big role here. So find some people who are willing to read and review your Kindle book. They can post the review on Amazon, or even on their personal blogs or websites, if they have any. This is a great way to ask a fellow blogger to review your book and write a post on it on their blog or a guest post on your blog. If you get any negative review, then be graceful about it and do not attack the reviewer. The key is to get as many reviews as possible, so that the word about your book reaches far and wide.

Create a website for the book

For a more focussed promotion of your Kindle book, one of the best ways can be to create a website focussing solely on the book. The website can be completely based on the book. You can add up additional features like newsletters, which the readers can sign up for and get for free. On this website, you can keep posting pictures of the book, reviews that the book may have received or any upcoming offer on the book. You can also include a discussion forum. This way, more and more people will get to know about your Kindle book and your promotional task will be done successfully.

GROWING YOUR KINDLE EMPIRE BY PUBLISHING MORE RELATED BOOKS

As we have discussed there was a time when becoming a published author would take years to be a reality. It would take months of going back and forth with publishing houses to get one book published. Well, the times have changed and with that, the possibilities have changed too.

Successful authors publish related books

Say you published your first ebook on Kindle and it becomes a runaway success. You will no doubt earn a lot of royalty. But, every day new books are being added to Kindle. It would only be a matter of time until your book fades away to the background and some other writer's book takes its place. This is why it is very important to keep being on the reader's radar. One way of doing this is by keep marketing about your book on various digital platforms like social networking sites and discussion forums. You can even start a website solely based on your book.

But, all the above efforts are bound to fizzle out after sometime. And you cannot really establish yourself as a writer in your reader's mind by publishing just on book. Hence, successful authors always move on to publish more books, which are in some way related to their first book.

Related books help the audience to recognise and connect

In order to be an established author, you have to have a decent number of books to your name. Writing related books to add on to your list of published books gives you that credential. When you write related books and publish them, they come up more often when the readers search for books of the particular genre. So, instead of depending on one book to catch your reader's eye, you will have multiple books. This will put the odds in your favour.

Also, having related books establishes you as a writer of that particular genre or topic. This means that your readers start connecting you with that genre and hence whenever they want to read a book of that genre, they would look you up, or recommend you to friends. It is very important to establish such connection in your reader's mind as that will substantially lead to multiple sale of your books on Kindle.

Then there is also the matter of earning more royalty. It is no surprise, that, the more books you have on Kindle store, more will be your chances of earning a good monthly or annual figure.

Instead of depending on flow of royalty from one book, you will be getting it from multiple books. This way you can really build up your Kindle book empire and become an established and high earning published author. It can also help you in your marketing efforts if you have a separate blog or website – thereby multiplying your earnings.

WHERE IS KINDLE PUBLISHING HEADING IN THE FUTURE?

Kindle books vs hard copy books – the present reality

The present scenario of Kindle books is extremely positive. It is a fact that hard copy books will never really go out of style. But, thanks to devices like Kindle, the demand for ebooks are on an all time high. The sales for print books have come down considerably, compared to the last decade and the sale of ebooks are breaking all records. Since most of the world population remains active on the digital platform, it is easy to see why they would want to opt for the conveninece of ebooks. These books can be easily browsed through and bought on the Kindle store and be read on the digital device anywhere. These ebooks do not take up any physical storage space either. So, they will remain to be a popular option among buyers.

As for the Kindle publishers, the market has never been this good. They are opting for Kindle publishing due to numerous reasons.

The biggest advantage of Kindle publishing lies in the fact that you will not have to be at the mercy of publishing houses to get your book published. So you do not lose unnecessary time and money over such publishing efforts. You can publish your book in Kindle, with all the formatting and editing done, in under an hour! There is also the added advantage of being able to reach a wider reader base within a short time. Kindle by itself is a highly established ebook reading platform with a huge number of users. The moment you publish a book on Kindle, it becomes accessible to thousands of readers around the world - that too within hours of publishing it on Kindle.

The future of Kindle publishing

There is no denying the fact that printed books will never be obsolete. There will always be book lovers who love the physical sensation of holding a book and building a collection. But, with the rapid spread and further development of technology, it can be safely assumed that the sale of ebooks and development of self publishing portals like Kindle will be on the rise too. To put it succinctly, Kindle publishing is probably heading towards a prosperous future.

CONCLUSION

Kindle provides many opportunities for individuals, authors and publishers - and it looks as though the Kindle phenomenon is here to stay.

As we have discussed, Kindle provides many advantages over traditional publishing. Put simply, it has never before in history been easier to publish books than it is today. What's more Kindle makes it easy to reach a potential worldwide audience in record time.

As you can see, one of the cornerstones of success with Kindle is picking good topics for books. Whilst that's definitely true it's also important that you just get on with it! Many people before you have felt so overwhelmed and confused by making the decision of what to create a book on that they have never gotten any further with their Kindle venture.

Whilst there are no guarantees of success with Kindle (there never is with any business) I hope you're exciting by the potential opportunities that Kindle provides you with.

I hope you found this book useful and I wish you much success!